Catching a Robber

Steve Gibson

DeafEducate

Two boys were walking down the road. Their names were Brian and Simon. They were talking.

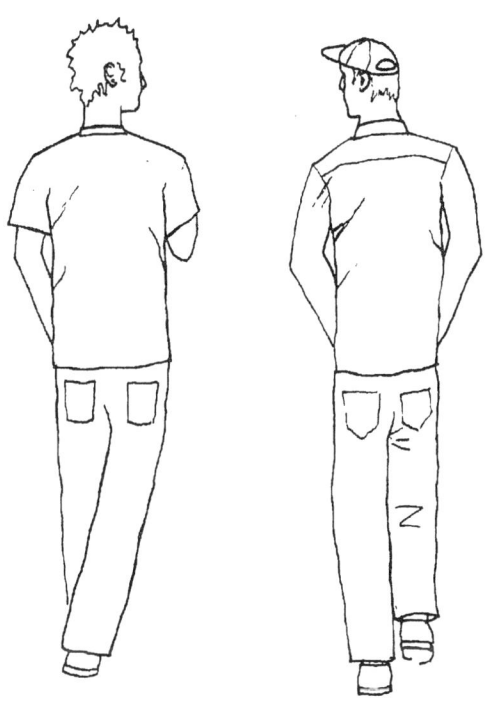

Simon said, "I saw 'Die Hard 2' last night on TV. It was good." Brian said, "Yes, it was ... Look! See that man."

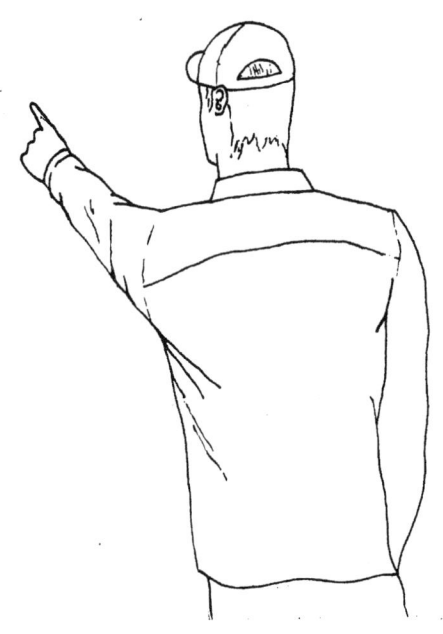

They saw a robber standing by a jewellery shop. He had a brick in his hand. The robber wore a striped jumper and a cap.

Brian and Simon saw him throwing the brick at the jewellery shop window. The window broke into bits. The robber took watches from the shop.

Brian said, "Simon, let's stop him!"
Simon said, "Yes, let's run."

They ran after the robber. The robber was shocked. He ran away. He dropped the brick and the watches.

Brian and Simon jumped on the robber. His cap fell away from his head. Brian grabbed the robber's hair. Simon held to his arm. The robber looked hurt.

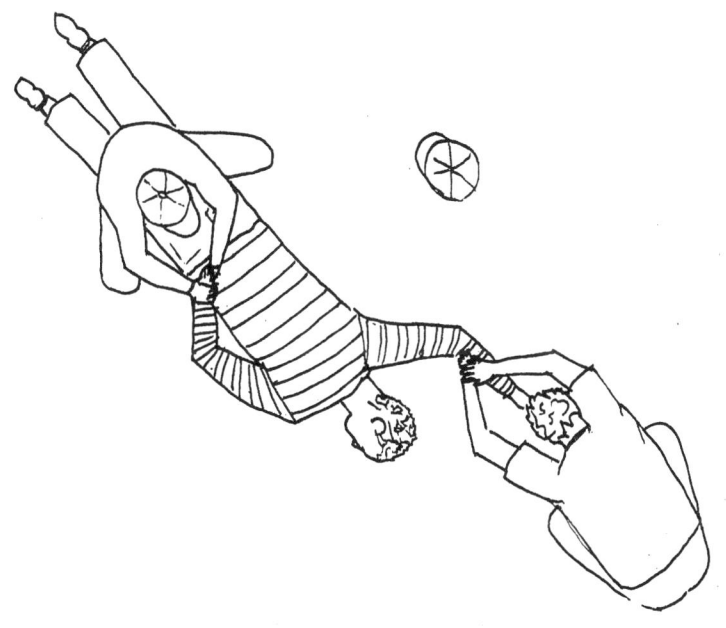

Suddenly, the boys heard people laughing. A woman and two men were laughing. Simon and Brian were puzzled and let the robber go.

Suddenly, the boys heard people laughing. A woman and two men were laughing. Simon and Brian were puzzled and let the robber go.

A policeman came to them and told them off.
He said to Brian and Simon, "Tsk, tsk, tsk, you have spoiled the film shooting. Look!"
The policeman pointed to the film crew.

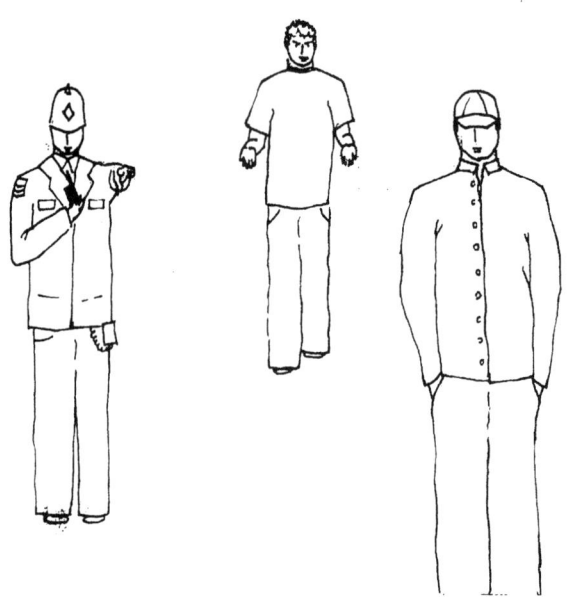

The cameraman was scowling. The director was angry and waved his hands about. The lighting man giggled quietly.

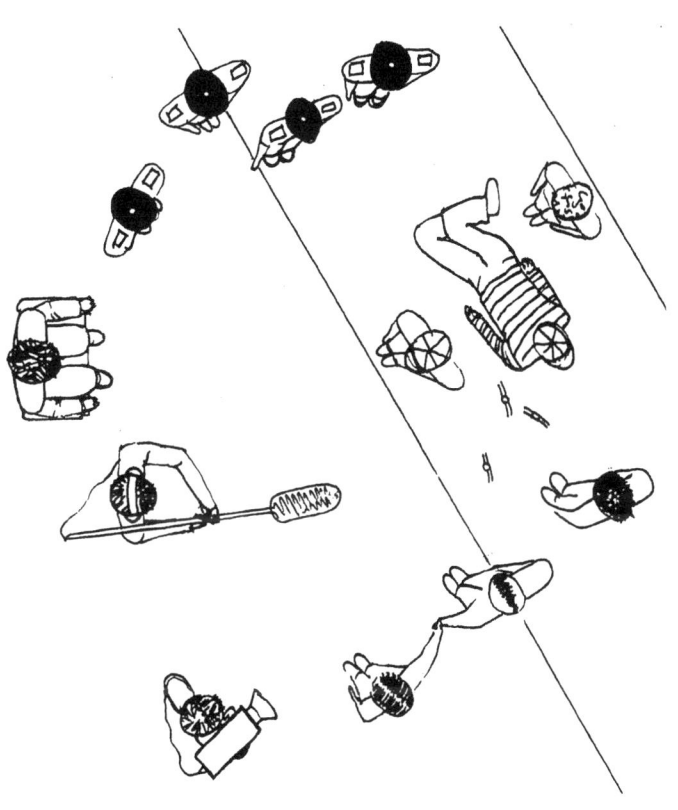

System Specifications

Operating system:
- Windows 98
- Windows ME
- Windows 2000
- Windows XP

Screen Resolution: 1024 x 768 pixels

Troubleshooting

When the CD is loaded, it should autorun.
But if it does not autorun, then do the following:

Click	*Start*
Click	*My Computer*
Double Click	eBook CD Drive

Then it should work.

For any other problems,

Visit www.deafeducation.co.uk
Click Troubleshooting at bottom of page